A Crabtree Branches Book

B. Keith Davidson

School-to-Home Support for Caregivers and Teachers

This high-interest book is designed to motivate striving students with engaging topics while building fluency, vocabulary, and an interest in reading. Here are a few questions and activities to help the reader build upon his or her comprehension skills.

Before Reading:

- *What do I think this book is about?*
- *What do I know about this topic?*
- *What do I want to learn about this topic?*
- *Why am I reading this book?*

During Reading:

- *I wonder why...*
- *I'm curious to know...*
- *How is this like something I already know?*
- *What have I learned so far?*

After Reading:

- *What was the author trying to teach me?*
- *What are some details?*
- *How did the photographs and captions help me understand more?*
- *Read the book again and look for the vocabulary words.*
- *What questions do I still have?*

Extension Activities:

- *What was your favorite part of the book? Write a paragraph on it.*
- *Draw a picture of your favorite thing you learned from the book.*

TABLE OF CONTENTS

What Does a Police Dog Do?

Police dogs have been around since the 1300s. They were used for both their strong noses and their ability to protect their handlers.

Night watchmen all across Europe used dogs to guard castle gates and city streets.

DENMARK
UNITED KINGDOM
NETHERLANDS
Ghent
BELGIUM
GERMANY
FRANCE
SWITZERLAND

FACT The first official K9 unit was formed in Ghent, Belgium, in 1899.

Police dogs have many different jobs. Some **patrol**, some are used to attack, and others are used to sniff out **contraband**.

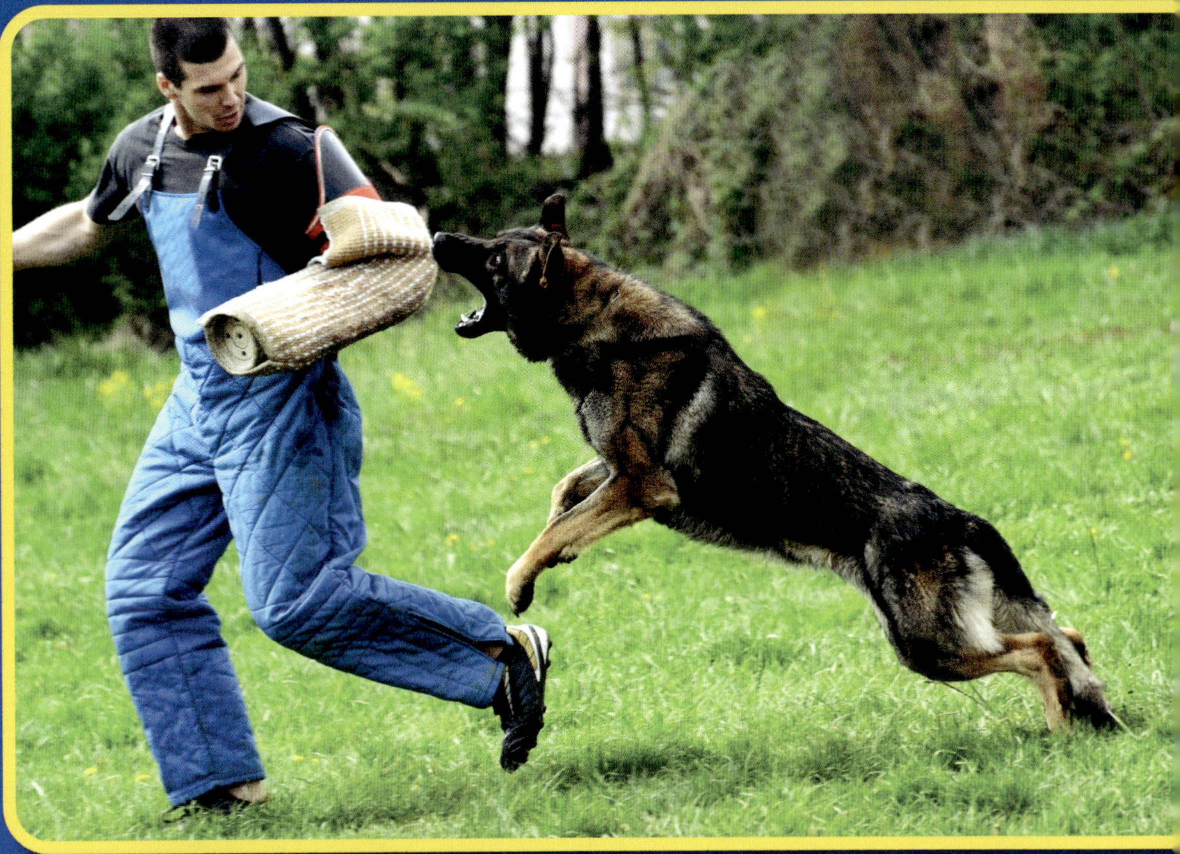

Many police dogs can perform multiple jobs. For example, some work as both **tracking** and protection dogs.

FACT

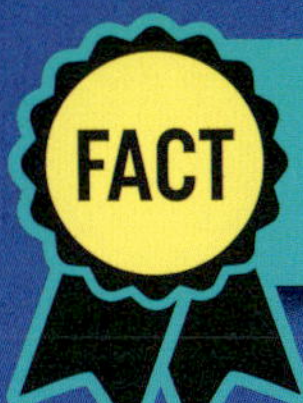

K9 is a term used by most police dog units. It relates to the Latin word for dog, canine.

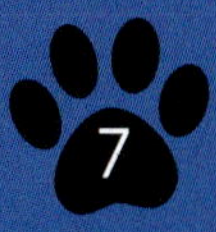

Police dogs are known for their powerful sense of smell. With their noses, the dogs search for contraband, pieces of evidence, and lost or missing persons.

They can also be trained to find guns, bullets, and electronic devices.

Many police departments give their dogs the official rank of “officer.”

Serving the Community

Police dogs work every day to keep our communities safe. These K9 officers are especially important during big events, such as sports games and marathons.

Bomb-sniffing dogs are often deployed to these events to search for **suspicious** packages.

The world's smallest police dog was a Chihuahua/Rat Terrier mix named Midge. She was 11 inches (28 cm) tall and 23 inches (58 cm) long.

The Ultimate Police Dog

The German shepherd is the dog people often associate with police work. They have the size and speed needed for capturing criminals.

German shepherd

Combine their size, speed, and powerful noses with their keen minds and learning abilities, and you can see why German shepherds are the ultimate police dogs.

Having a police dog on the scene often stops a situation from getting out of hand. Criminals don't want to fight these dogs.

Sniffing Dogs

Beagles are a smaller breed. They would have trouble taking down a large human, but they know how to follow their noses. They are commonly used as **detection** dogs. They search for explosives, evidence, or contraband.

Beagle

Bloodhound

Bloodhounds are also used only for their noses. These kinds of police dogs are called single-purpose police dogs.

FACT
Cadaver dogs sniff around for human remains. They are around 95% accurate.

Other Breeds

The Belgian Malinois and Dutch shepherd are smaller cousins of the German shepherd. They are quickly becoming popular police dogs.

Belgian Malinois

Dutch shepherd

Belgian Malinois

Their smaller size makes them more **agile** than their bigger cousins, and they can keep up in the intelligence department, too.

Some police dogs are given metal teeth. These are not used as weapons, however. They are used to protect the dog's teeth.

Picking the Perfect Puppy

Police dogs are chosen only after they've been through an obedience school's program. Most are picked and trained as puppies. Others are picked from shelters and may be older dogs.

Police dogs must show that they will listen without hesitation. The initial training lasts 10 to 12 weeks, but a police dog never stops improving its skills.

A well-trained police dog can save police departments 600 to 1000 **man-hours** every year.

Police dogs live with their handlers while on the job. They become regular members of the family in their new households. This strengthens the bond between the working partners. After the dog retires, it usually stays living with its handler.

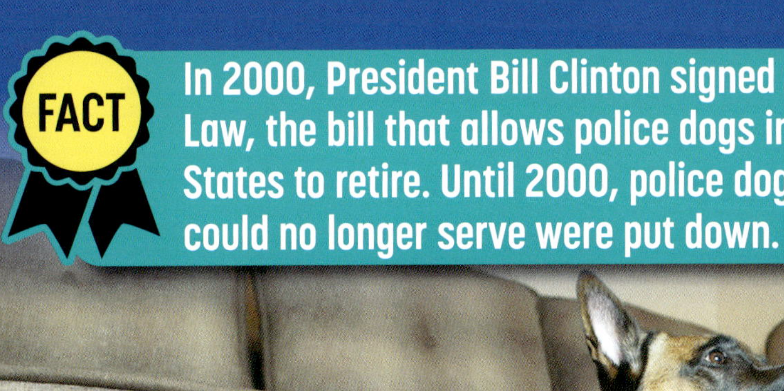

FACT

In 2000, President Bill Clinton signed Robby's Law, the bill that allows police dogs in the United States to retire. Until 2000, police dogs that could no longer serve were put down.

Training

Training a police dog isn't just about the dog. It is also about finding the right handler, or partner. The handler first has to complete the police academy. Then, they spend a few years working as an officer before being considered for the K9 program.

Training for a police dog and its handler never really ends. They devote as much as 500 hours to training each year.

Some people think that police dogs are trained in different languages so that criminals can't give them **commands**. The truth is, police dogs use the same commands that a regular dog would. However, a police dog listens only to its handler.

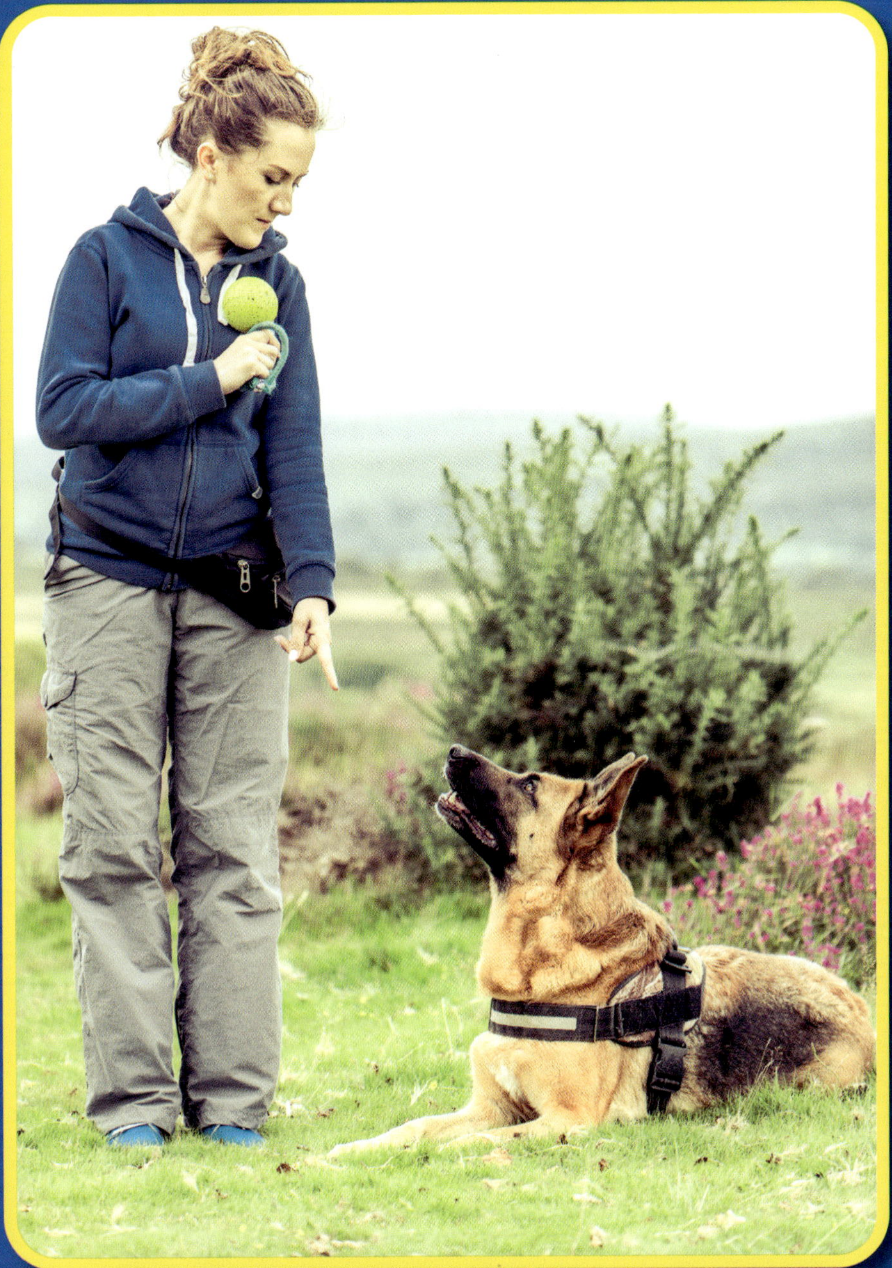

FACT

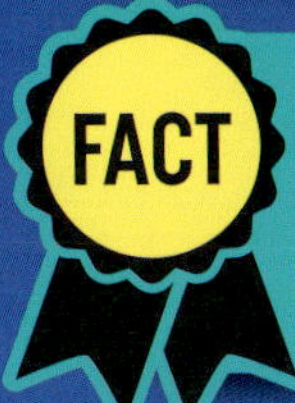

Even if the handler has an identical twin, the dog will know the difference. Dogs know humans by their unique smells.

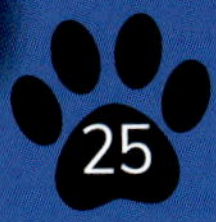

Police Dogs are Heroes!

When the planes crashed into the twin towers of the World Trade Center on September 11, 2001, police dogs were on the scene. These dogs helped save people from the wreckage.

They could smell through the layers of rubble and direct rescue crews to people who were trapped.

Police dogs are trained to do incredible things. Every year, there are awards given to police dogs that go above and beyond.

In 2017, a 3-year-old German shepherd won an award for jumping off of a 30-foot-high (9.14 meter-high) wall to chase a **suspect**.

Every day, all over the world, police dogs serve and protect their communities.

Glossary

agile (Aj-il): the ability to move quickly and easily

cadaver (KUH-da-ver): a dead body

commands (kuh-MANDZ): orders given to a person or animal

contraband (KON-truh-band): illegal substances, products, or devices

detection (di-TEKT-shuhn): the act or process of finding something that is hidden

man-hours (MAN-ourz): the amount of work that a human can do in one hour

patrol (puh-TROHL): the process of monitoring an area. When police officers are out on the streets, they're on patrol.

suspect (suh-SPEKT): a person who is thought to have committed a crime

suspicious (suh-SPISH-uhss): something questionable, dishonest, or dangerous in character

tracking (TRAK-ing): the process of following a person or animal as they move

Index

Websites to Visit

https://kids.kiddle.co/Police_dog

https://easyscienceforkids.com/all-about-police-dogs/

https://www.ducksters.com/animals/policedogs.php

About the Author

B. Keith Davidson

B. Keith Davidson grew up around dogs and has always been fascinated by the bonds that humans and these very special creatures share. Beagles are his favorite dogs, even if they are stubborn and frustrating. He has a Master's degree in Canadian History from Carleton University.

Written by: B. Keith Davidson
Designed by: Jennifer Dydyk
Edited by: Kelli Hicks
Proofreader: Janine Deschenes

Photographs: Cover illustration of Dog(also on title page) © Nevada3, photo of city © ssguy, photo of police officer © XiXinXing, photo of dog © NSC Photography, Page 5 castle © Cimmerian, dog © Morphart Creation, map © seamuss, Page 6 © YAKOBCHUK VIACHESLAV, Page 7 © muroPhotographer, Page 8 © Photographer Dubnytskaya, Page 10 bottom photo © Photo Spirit, Page 11 © Fuss Sergey, Page 13 top photo © wideweb, Page 14 © New Africa, Page 15 top photo © Lenkadan, bottom photo © Noska Photo, Page 16 top photo © DragoNika, bottom photo © Viktorija Zar, Page 17 © Grisha Bruev, Page 19 top photo © Dale A Stork, Page 22 © Victor Jiang, Page 27 inset photo © Leeloona, Page 29 © John Roman Images. All images from Shutterstock.com except the following from istock by Getty Images: Page 4 © aijohn784, Page 9 © Sergei Ginak, Page 10 top photo © casiano, Page 12 © steved_np3, Page 13 bottom photo © SergeyTikhomirov, Page 18 © Barb, Page 19 bottom photo and Page 21 top photo © yacobchuk, Page 20 © Ibrakovic, Page 21 bottom photo © Eudyptula, Page 23 © JRLPhotographer, Page 24 © sssss1gmel, Page 25 © merc67. The large image across Page 26 and 27 courtesy of The Library of Congress, Page 28 © Cynoclub | Dreamstime.com

Library and Archives Canada Cataloguing in Publication

CIP available at Library and Archives Canada

Library of Congress Cataloging-in-Publication Data

CIP available at Library of Congress

Crabtree Publishing Company

www.crabtreebooks.com 1-800-387-7650

 Printed in the U.S.A./CG20210915/012022

 In Canada: We acknowledge the financial support of the Government of Canada through the Canada Book Fund for our publishing activities.

Published in the United States
Crabtree Publishing
347 Fifth Avenue, Suite 1402-145
New York, NY, 10016

Published in Canada
Crabtree Publishing
616 Welland Ave.
St. Catharines, Ontario L2M 5V6